The Love Song
of Laura Ingalls Wilder

The
Love Song
of
Laura Ingalls Wilder

Sharon McCartney

NIGHTWOOD EDITIONS
Gibsons Landing, BC

The characters in this book are the product of fancy; any resemblance, in whole or in part, to any person, living or dead, is unintentional.

Nightwood Editions
773 Cascade Crescent
Gibsons, BC, Canada V0N 1V9
www.nightwoodeditions.com

Cover design by Anna Comfort
Printed and bound in Canada

Nightwood Editions acknowledges
financial support from the Government
of Canada through the Canada Council
for the Arts and the Book Publishing
Industry Development Program (BPIDP),
and from the Province of British
Columbia through the British Columbia
Arts Council, for its publishing activities.

THE CANADA COUNCIL | LE CONSEIL DES ARTS
FOR THE ARTS | DU CANADA
SINCE 1957 | DEPUIS 1957

BRITISH
COLUMBIA
ARTS COUNCIL
Supported by the Province of British Columbia

Library and Archives Canada Cataloguing in Publication

McCartney, Sharon, 1959–
    The love song of Laura Ingalls Wilder / Sharon McCartney.

Poems.
ISBN 978-0-88971-233-1

    1. Wilder, Laura Ingalls, 1867–1957—Poetry. I. Title.
PS8575.C427L69 2007   C811'.54   C2007-901556-5

For Martin, Kelly and Gabriel

Contents

Foreword

What follows is a series of poems that relies for its inspiration on the children's books of Laura Ingalls Wilder, the "Little House" books. While the poems use the voices of characters (human and non-human, animate and inanimate) from the books, I don't think of them as being an extension of Wilder's stories. Rather, the voices, the characters and the details are vehicles, a way to say what I want to say.

What attracts me to the Little House books as source material is the contrast between the author's romantic version of her family's experiences on the American frontier of the 1880s and the reality. The books are seen by many as purely factual reminiscences of pioneer life. The author and her daughter (Rose Wilder Lane, who is credited by some as having a major role in writing and/or editing the books) vehemently defended the books' authenticity in their lifetimes.

Yet, the Little House books are creative works. Wilder and Lane manipulated facts, condensed characters and eliminated unpleasant episodes. There is no mention of the family's brief tenure as innkeepers in Iowa or of the death of the only male infant in the family at nine months of age. In *The Long Winter*, the narrative celebrates the family's heroics in surviving, yet ignores the lifelong damage from what is thought to be rickets one of the daughters suffered due to their dismal diet.

Wilder's life after the period described by the Little House books also invites examination. The Wilder farm in Missouri was for many years barely more than marginal. Rose Wilder Lane wrote later of her "malnutrition" childhood in a log cabin. Almanzo, Wilder's husband, describes his life as having been "mostly disappointments" in a late letter to Lane. Neither Lane nor her mother ever acknowledged the contribution Lane made to the books.

But these poems are not meant to reveal anything about Wilder's life or the lives of the characters, many of whom were real people, in her books. The books are fascinating relics that I find myself returning to at least yearly, but the poems in this series are my own.

Ma

Ma had been very fashionable, before she married Pa, and a
dressmaker had made her clothes.
                    – *Little House in the Big Woods*

This morning I addressed the roof beams,
Charles twitching in sleep beside me:
Today I will do whatever I want.

That lasted until sun-up. Duty dresses itself as
what I want—sifting, wiping, straining
toward cheerfulness which becomes, daily miracle,
cheerfulness. The children don't know.
They believe what they hear.

Sometimes I want to gather that black crepe
and burn it in a heap. Walk back to Concord
in my green delaine. Never thread
a needle again.

                    I try to cultivate an aura
of elegance, decorum. But to be well-bred
means to be in hand. Not blind-sided. Not
bushwhacked, not weeping over the well cover
so no one will see.

How many earthen floors have I swept?
How many silty streams have I drunk from?

If only Freddy had lived, things would be
different. How still he was on the table, as if
his soul had vacated, abandoned a claim,
left only lumber, bare sod, debris.

Our world no more than the dried mud and wisps
that God, standing at the pantry door,
whisks to the wind.

Freddy, Dead at Nine Months

They never knew what he died of; he just sickened and
wasted away and died.
                              – Rose Wilder Lane, *A Little House Sampler*

Ma gathers me up, disbelieving,
calls to me as if I sleep, presses her ear
to my chest, her finger to my lips,
pricks the soles of my feet,
unconvinced.

They bury me behind Peter's house,
a ragtag procession. August, Minnesota,
autumn already staining the maples.
Such an object of pity they bundle me
in woollens. Lumber on to Iowa.

Sometimes Ma, in her extremity,
weeping privately over the washtub,
senses my presence, feels that I'm near,
calls herself a fool. But she's not mistaken.
I *am* there behind the stove. I am the heat
on her brow, my privilege to tarry,
suffered to loiter as I couldn't in life,
moonbeam, magpie, gust in the slough.

I'm not alone as she fears, nor unhappy.
No chip on my ineffable shoulder. Rather
a rich air of communion, buoyance—what
you feel when your heart swells. And
there *they* are—Ma, my sisters, isolated,
stragglers, each with her own reduction:
should have been me, could have been me.
Staggered, drifting, aimless as cattle
in a blizzard, heads lowered, numb,
the horizon hopelessly obscured.

Jack, Swept Away When the River Rises Suddenly Mid-Ford

They had forgotten Jack.

– Little House on the Prairie

Do they stop? Do I even get a backward glance when the water
catches me in its teeth, drags me downstream? Like scrabbling
in bedrock, sleep-chasing a hare, splashing in mad perpendicular
circles, around boulders, through lathery catacombs, under urine-
streaked tablelands, past deer dozing in heat-hazy bottoms, lifting
languid crowns. It's all I can do to keep my nose up, courage
sneaking away, froth ringing my muzzle, but then the river widens
and slows, drops to its knees, an overworked mustang, blowing.
I stagger into bluestem, cough a weed, legs wobbly as a colt's,
rest long enough to dry my lungs, then upstream on the banks.
One mile? Two? Sun dropping, their trail beyond the ford easy
enough, leathery pony-scent, nose-wrinkling soap, that hunk
of salt pork in a jar like a chain at my throat as I jog the wheel-
track, snapping at black flies, chiggers, irritations, the incontinent
discontent that shadows me. All my years of fawning, begging
scraps, reconnoitring the barnyard, footpads frost-burnt, sounding
out danger, wolves, panthers, coons in the corncrib, for naught.
What a fool I was. Younger, the sight of them thrilled me, the man,
the woman. I curled to absorb their smell, but fondness fades,
as does energy, a history of wearying grudges, injustices, yardful
of half-buried femurs. To quit them and starve? My legs know
better, the tail that betrays me. I'm hungry, nothing to gnaw but
my dismay at their unterritorial wandering, unwilling to stick
to a place. I locate them at last, bedded down for the night,

ponies tethered, but he comes at me with the gun, alarmed.
I make myself small, abased, crawl on my belly, my obeisance
made manifest, my servility. I swallow the shame of his mistake,
my gratitude a sheathed fang.

Mary, Blinded After Scarlet Fever

Now she could not see even the brightest light any more. She was still patient and brave.

– By the Shores of Silver Lake

Swallows coursing red river bluffs, cottonwoods,
the autumn garden, pumpkins and squash like strands
of amber unloosed in clay, gone, first to fog,
brown flour sifting, then spilled ink, charred flint,
ashes where a palace once sprawled.
How is the gold become dim!

I'm told I am lucky, but I doubt. If my eyes,
then why not my ears? I wake up wondering
what faculty will fail today, dread like a cloud
on the horizon, prairie fire, locusts, blizzard,
twister, fear beating its tom-tom by the river.

Kindness irks me, scratchy woolens, hoppers
underfoot. I want to shout—Laura's meek
gloating, Ma's hush, Pa unnatural, solicitous—
I hate their wholeness, their health, so much
I don't know what to do with my hands. And God?
Old pole-cat. Indian-giver. From a basket of rags,
I weave a plait as taut as my nerves.

This is a train they'll never ride. Think of Lazarus.
Is this how he felt when the rock rolled away? He had
begun his journey, but Christ collared him, tore his ticket,
tossed his carpetbag from the rack. If he complained,
it was only to himself for who would commiserate?
Thoughtless stunt, using Lazarus for a lesson which
leaves him an oddity, a wayfarer, puzzling why,
unlike all others, he must die twice.

Charlotte

Then a terrible thing happened. Anna would not give up
Charlotte.

– On the Banks of Plum Creek

This is not what I wanted. Every evening in my box,
my prayer was please God make something happen,
renewal, bounty, a new frock, calico done over, fresh
yarn curls, a rag man, perhaps, to tease. What I got
was Anna, sticky neighbour child, fat, blonde, bawling,
my role to appease. Enchanted by my black button
eyes, she squeezed, refused to surrender, stomped and
fumed, and they threw up their hands, knuckled under.
Where was God? Must hope always be extinguished?
My world withered in an instant, desiccated, mauled,
dandled over the wagon's lip, then disengaged, jettisoned,
Anna distracted, dropped me in a slushy wheel rut.
A minor catastrophe overall. Folly to assume that I matter.
My rag doll arms, legs, heart, precious as they are to me
no more than scraps to my maker, snippets, trimmings.
Pieced together by chance, whim, undone the same way,
night coalescing, spring rain that soddened my joints,
stitching, stuff and batten, stiffening now to ice.

China Shepherdess

Older still, older than Laura could remember, Ma's china
shepherdess stood pink and white and smiling on the shelf.
                                    – *Little Town on the Prairie*

My life up to now as false as the gabled storefronts
of Calumet Avenue, as my pink enamelled smile.
I was never anything more than décor. How could
I have been so clay-headed? In the kiln, I burned
with the heat of creation, restless, craving adventure.
I acquiesced gracefully to boxes and crates. I was
rolled in quilts, face-down among soulless cups and
saucers, traversing Wisconsin, Dakota, the Verdigris,
in unsprung wagons with scathing cutlery to grace
the what-not of a jerry-built shanty, a signifier of
the eastern city I came from, of fashion, vanities.
I tried hard, hiked my rucked-up skirts in an attitude
to please, simpered my gilt slippers daintily, though
I would have preferred hobnails, coveralls, a kerchief
for my locks, a flock in the lea. Where is my shepherd?
Where are my sheep? Nothing to keep me from wagging
tails, clumsy elbows sweeping the shelf of delft and blue
willow, dust and trinkets, launching us, feckless nestlings,
into the inside-out nakedness of shattered love.

Black Susan

The little log house had changed hands several times and now it was a corncrib, but nothing would persuade that cat to live anywhere else.

– By the Shores of Silver Lake

Once I was everything, my mother's world,
her striate tongue all over me, soothing the emptiness
in my chest. Gazing at her, black iridescence, fingerling
hints of gold, hazel eyes, how afraid I was that she
would die—how would I survive?

Soon I was restless, ticking, sick of her narrow-hearted
bossing, cuffs and hisses, politics—predators everywhere!—
her strictures, spitting. All I wanted was out, a mate.
A relentless impatience.

                        A cabin in the woods.
Insinuated myself. Saucers of cream when the cow
was wet. Curds, parings, barn replete with rodents.
Even the dog was pleasant, sharing the stone hearth,
my mother's theory disproven. Livestock shifting
narcotically in their stalls, numerous lookouts, hayloft,
rail fence. Suffering the children, strings and teasings,
yet ever an undercurrent, a purr of discontent. I needed
them, their clumsy angularity, lack of sense.

Then they vamoosed. With the dog. I wasn't worried.
Give me shelter, a handout, I'll take it, but surely
I could do without.

           The truth is it's hard, hard, hard
on my own. Prey is remarkably devilish, snoring
deep under tree roots, unreachable. Frostbitten ears,
days without meat, always a fresh litter of mewlings.

Self-reliance has its rewards, but they're meagre.
Solitude. Insularity. Occupying the fringes, never
the uneasy centre of attention, the petted. No demeaning
debt of gratitude. No expectations. Warm nights alone
in the bowels of a corncrib.

Nellie Oleson

"My goodness!" Mary said. "I couldn't be as mean as that
Nellie Oleson."

         – On the Banks of Plum Creek

Skin as white as strychnine, noose of French lace,
tortoiseshell comb. Critiquing my coif in the vanity
glass, I come unsettled, pulse awry. Where do I
begin and end? My composure jumping the banks,
raw current, impulse, oscillating signal that gallops
telegraph wires, scalloped rooming house steps,
into fog frozen in riverbank willows, into flagstones,
boardwalks, the icy mud that mires the ostler's dray.

Am I alone too often? So my former friends
say—their horrid hovering, leech-like. I cast off
Miss Bell, Miss Humphrey, Mr. Frank as I did
my bustles and hoops. As I did the slapdash avenues
of De Smet, Dakota, my mother and father, half-baked
failure-mongers, forever favouring dim-witted Willie.
Must one be an idiot to be loved?

Connection, interaction—once I cultivated these,
but only in my power to lord, to railroad, a coup
to reduce impertinent Miss Ingalls—patched calico
and braids—to fury, sniffles, stamping a bare foot
in dust. Amity eluded me, how effortlessly gaggling
schoolgirls brayed their affection, linking arms.
Envious, I indulged in the succor of melodrama, pap,
imagined that the hurt I suffered when shunned
mirrored that of, say, Mr. Cooley, his boy and mule
whirled off by a twister, every bone snapped.

Now older, I impart an air of removal, refinement,
to the milliner's counter, aquiline nose upturned as thick-
waisted matrons count out coppers. Thursday evening,
at a temperance meeting, I sit mildly, thoughts spiralling
into the rafters, away from pinched armpits, a headache,
hollowness in my chest, as if my heart were drafty,
an eyesore, tarpaper, tin, ramshackle.

Mr. Edwards

He bowed to Ma and called her "Ma'am," politely. But he
told Laura he was a wildcat from Tennessee.
– Little House on the Prairie

Time's not a line but a whip, snapping,
the insult I thought long-forgotten
regenerating: Lucille, whom I fancied,
jesting that she would require two domiciles
at least, five acres with outbuildings,
to tolerate being yoked to me. I lit out,
no hankering for spitfires, opted
for solitude, homesteading, Kansas,
the prairie a plateau of burdens, low hills,
wild mustard, a buffalo wallow grown over.
Like fishing a jar of bad luck: grass fires,
drought, hail, claim-jumpers, horse-thieves,
wolves as bold as Lucille. As toothy.
A spiteful climate, chin cocked, chippy.
Blizzard nights, wind-addled, swaddled
in a saddle blanket, jawing with the stove,
conjuring a woman, powdery brown skin
of a tuber roasted in ash. Regret? That's
just living in the past. Adam lost a rib,
a permanent part of himself, to loneliness.

Ma's Green Delaine Dress

The delaine was kept wrapped in paper and laid away.
   – Little House in the Big Woods

The sugaring-off, liberated from the trunk,
how I whirled and twirled, sweat-gilded,
skirt flirting insatiably, whalebone stays
taut with glee. One sweet odyssey of display,
a chance to be worn, to adorn, after such
loneliness, confinement, wrapped in stiff paper.

Why don't we dance every night? Flounced
and ruffled, trimmed with ribbon, fashioned
for pleasure. What makes her pack me away?
Misguided notion that joy must be rationed.

In darkness, fear unfolds. A finite future—
she can't see my seams are weakening, how
my tucks and gathers fray. Styles change.
Before she knows it, I'll be passé, fodder
for the dressmaker's scissors, revamped—
or worse, remade into curtains, an apron,
common workaday pieces, a rag
to wipe greasy lips on.

Pa's Big Green Book

And they all sat on the floor together and looked at the
pictures in the Bible, and the pictures of all kinds of animals
and birds in Pa's big green book.

– Little House in the Big Woods

Why are you so unreliable, haphazard,
unpredictable? So disappointing?
I don't know how to read you. You
pull me down, amiable, pore over me
in the amber kerosene light, then shun
me for weeks. You forget about me.
Why are you so changeable?

I'm always here, always the same. I
mean what I say. Spine straight, forthright,
looking at you. I've never been able to lie.
Never been able to hide how I feel.

So many books on the shelf. You're bored.
I'm too old. Do you think you know
what I'm about? Think again. There's
an edge to each sheet of paper.

I turn my thoughts inward, to coloured
plates of tropical oddities, exotics,
green and yellow plumage, banana
trees, coconut fronds, steamy air that
would curl my pages, leave me panting
in dampness like a played-out dog.

At least I have that—reverie, daydreams.
The last night you held me becomes
an illustration I flip back to. Each time,
a shadow, a brushstroke, a ghostly
face in the clouds, dissolving.

Uncle George's Bugle

Laura had never seen a wild man before. She did not know
whether she was afraid of Uncle George or not.
– *Little House in the Big Woods*

Nothing pleased me more than to dangle
sidelong, jolting toward the moment when
he would purse his lips, exhale his call
to arms into me.

          I loved his combativeness,
rough grip lifting, pointing me cloudward,
the way my voice galloped with his wind
inside me. I was content to be suborned,
the two of us exhorting the charge, blaring
orisons, the horses answering.

But that was the war and the war is done.

He wanders now, at a loss, idle. His brothers
shake their heads, lament his wildness,
wish him gone.

As for me, I have no role.
Slung over the bedpost by a tattered sash.
My best days behind me. A hanger-on.

Unfair of me to require so much, that he should
transport me, deliver me, through bullets, sabres,
wresting a song from my emptiness.

At the sugaring-off, he sips from a flask, rotgut,
sour mash, jigging. His lust renewed, he reaches
for me. Almost too much, to be tongued again,
pressure from his throat—in my voice,
an unfamiliar vibrato, a new melody
piercing the unpopulated woods.

Churn

Wash on Monday,
Iron on Tuesday,
Mend on Wednesday,
Churn on Thursday,
Clean on Friday,
Bake on Saturday,
Rest on Sunday.

– Little House in the Big Woods

Thursday tastes of sourness, curdling,
buckets of fresh cream dumped down
my neck, set by the stove to warm.
Then the bump, bump, bump of the dash
agitating my thoughts.

        Disturbances—
the broom's inconsiderate teasing,
meaningless caresses brushing my feet.
Incongruence, fracture, falsity, distress,
the flooding creek that divides what you
want or expect from what you are given.

All of this churns inside me, a restlessness,
as if I were pacing a small, bare room,
tracing a way out of disorder.

The mother falls back in her rocker, arm
sore, exhausted. The daughter steps up
for a turn. Gradually, the graining occurs.
What seems insurmountable becomes,
with each stroke, a beat in the past.
Richness coalesces, sunbright butter,
kneaded, moulded in a strawberry form.

The problem is never how to remember,
but how to forget, to transform rawness,
pain, eternal confusion into something
more appetizing, resolve, reconciliation,
the realization that softens winter's stark
brown loaf, unpalatable potatoes.

Pa's Rifle

It's not the bullet that kills you, as the song goes,
it's the hole.
– Charles Wright, "River Run"

I lose control. Say things I shouldn't.
Always the acrid cloud of regret
afterward. Those blunt colourless
thoughts that are best kept hidden.

If only I were like the churn, the broom,
or even the hatchet. Self-contained.
What's in me seems bound to burst out,
desires connection, always for worse.
Does anyone feel the way I do?
Loaded? Aimed? The slightest pressure,
a touch, a spark, sets me off. When
the swan swam into my sights—
I couldn't help the shout, the shot,
as always, noise, wounds,
a stiffening carcass.

Best to leave me over the door, at rest
on my pegs, out of reach. Don't run
a rag over my barrel, down the stock,
don't brush the trigger. When you pull,
even inadvertently, I can't help my
reaction. Think of the shame, how it
tears up my heart.

       Malevolence, pain—
it's not all my fault. Untouched, I'm
harmless, benign. In your hands,
disaster.

Pa's Ax

Then he took his gun, and slinging his ax on his shoulder he
went away to the clearing to cut down some more trees.
                                    – *Little House in the Big Woods*

Swing me and swing me—tell me the dance
will never end. No fatigue, no disinterest,
no mortal concerns. I was honed precisely
for this, to cut cleanly through secret places,
moist inner flesh of each trunk and limb and,
oh, I want more and more. Stubborn, damnable
oak, pimpled with knots, hickory, fir, poplar,
the tender, compliant birch shedding gossamer
bark. I don't know how to hold back, to say
enough is enough, turn away, lay my head
down on a stump. Isn't it better to act, even
to engender remorse, than to wonder what
might have been? I can't bear a weakness
as debilitating as rust, blistering my blade.
I was meant to thirst, to bite in parabolas
of desire. Wood was meant to fall.

The Stove Considers Pa

He had kindled the fire.

– The Long Winter

Each morning, he bows before me,
a bundle of kindling in his arms.
I am hollow. He lights the fire,
feeds it, and soon I'm ticking,
expansive, radiant heat migrating
from belly to stovetop to limbs.

He warms his hands, grinning,
pleased with what he has wrought.
No thought for me, what it is to burn
after abstinence, that my iron soul
might prefer to be dark, untended.
No one gathered around.

He sits close to me, conspiratorially,
then moves away. At night, my embers
banked, I smoulder, unhappy, petulant,
torn—I don't know what I want.
First: why does he ignore me?
Then: why doesn't he leave me alone?

By morning, I'm settled. Blackened,
but at peace. A comfortable chill.
I treasure those times, untroubled,
unstirred. Then he rises, bows
before me. We're at it again.

Pa's Penis

Get on your pony and ride.

— The Fleshtones

Pioneer, each night under the nine-patch,
I explore the territories, seek out the gap,
the mountain pass that opens with a sigh
to green coastal waters, salt dunes and pine.
Like burying my head in umber, wrapping
a blanket of mist around my shoulders.

By day, I loaf, lie abed, keep to myself.
Too shy to speak, ordinarily, to step out,
vulnerable. But in darkness, close quarters,
I make myself known, a feral growl,
the urge to go west, to penetrate,
ungovernable.

      On occasion, however,
I am denied. A barricade. Timbers blocking
the trail. Does anything hurt more than that?
To be willing, radiant, fresh and dandy,
and, then, to be stymied, impeded,
unhitched, turned away.

A deflating anger,
draining, at myself for my lack of control.
At the other, for what? Anything? To say
never again would be a lie; my tendency
is perennial, reseeding, bound to reoccur.
A buffoon, perhaps, wagging, overeager,
but my heart in the right place, on my sleeve,
incapable of disguise, concealment. Desire
made manifest, destiny.

The Log That Falls on Ma's Foot during Construction of the Little House

Pa was trying to hold up his end of it, to keep it from falling on Ma. He couldn't.

— *Little House on the Prairie*

Metronomic cycle of seasons chug-chugging—
the headache of summer, overindulgence.
Winter's wooden stare, chloroform, scalpel.
Wake up to April in tears, wanting so much
to live, to feel the earth softening, smiling,
a mild breeze in my new green bangles.

Then ruination. A man with an axe
roaming the copse, wagonload of corpses.
What I thought was my life truncated,
upended, denuded, shorn, roots orphaned,
telling their bitter story, how inherently
unlikeable I was.

Never a very good tree, I'll admit.
Unsuited to crowding, congregation,
the suffocating poke-bonnet foliage
of elders. But did I deserve this?

Things I never got a chance to do:
tell the holy barred owl to fuck off,
backhand the pestering flickers,
watch my offspring leaf out,
the frug, the swim, the hokey-pokey.

At the last, as I am hoisted heavenward,
supine, to my future as a wall,
a moment of abandon, desperation,
phantom pain in my hacked-off limbs.
I leap, their weakness an avenue,
roll and tumble, land on her small
black boot—her pitiable cry as fragile
as the voices of ferns. I am instantly
sorry. Even this is visited on me.

Covered Wagon

The wagon had been home for a long time.

– Little House on the Prairie

Both joy and torment—the memory
of what was: our weeks on the trail,
singing my wheel song in the grasses,
willow bows arched over my back,
a gown of white canvas. Constant
amusement, companionship, something
to do, inhabitants all around, horses tied
to the trough or hitched to my tongue,
bulldog sighing in the shade below.
Contentment, the prairie opening
its arms as we crest an upswelling—
I didn't know I could be so happy.

Is there a tonic, something to alleviate
my romantic foolishness? I'm not naive;
I've been around, but I always forget
that the journey must end. Reason
trumps passion. People inevitably
entertain interests other than me—
a handsome buggy, an underhanded plow.

Unloaded. Unpacked. Galling, to recall
I fetched cordwood for the hearth they
gather near. Once, they leaned close to me.
My heart splinters with emptiness.

Dust in my axles, fractures in my spokes,
the beginning of a breakdown. I'll work
again, loads of hay, excursions to town,
but it won't be the same—that felicity,
absolute love returned absolutely.

The Breaking Plow

Pa had a new plow, a breaking plow. It was wonderful for
breaking the prairie sod.
— *Little Town on the Prairie*

My cutting wheel leads, slicing a vein
for the fluted plowshare. A roller of sod
uncurls, a wave devolving.

If only remorse could be turned so easily.
I get carried away by the persuasion
of horses, harness, Pa's compulsion.
At the end of the row, the team pivots;
I'm faced with the scene. Bucolic really.
Blackbirds descending in my wake to pick
morsels. A feast of corpses.

                                    The grasses'
ancient discourse disrupted, torn. Diaspora
of jackrabbit, prairie dog, garter snake, worm.

Then long uneventful nights in the barn. I miss
the whetted blade ripping, my wooden frame
riding that keen edge.

                    Time creates consequences.
The next day and the next. I want to plow
in the moment, act on impulse, no thought
for tomorrow, for what others might think.

But that's not the world in which I was forged.
Hear the brood hen's cluck-clucking.
The hog's jaded snort.

Put the earth under me and I will dig in.
I'm not saying I'm blameless.
I'm just saying I know.

The Lone Cottonwood

There's a microsecond of inconceivable pain, Baxter Jack
guesses, and if you pass out on the way down the impact is
dreamlike, but hurts twice as much.
                                        – Levi Dronyk, "Baxter Jack"

Quiet mornings, a beauty that subdues,
renders the blackbirds reverent.
Gentler now, easier to be alone, none
of the uproar of youth, the grove.
Room to think, to stretch my petioles,
craning on tiptoes to glimpse the train,
its boiled breath, avuncular coughs,
bisecting the prairie billows. From the town
that mushroomed overnight comes
the dreadful racket of sawing, hammers,
haunting, like the memories that breach
my furrowed skin:

                Levi, so handsome,
darker than most, deceptive, charming—
a smile that was always illicit—the first
to go. I still see him shimmering in wind,
each move suggestive, concussive, the rest
of us envious, admiring.

Is hope a comfort for some? What happens
when it is felled?

The others followed in steady succession,
stout, blooming siblings trundled off
as logs, seedlings withered, overcome
by sickness. Now I am lone, but not lonely.
Sad, but not desperate. Why was I spared?
Grateful to be alive for as long as it lasts,
my feet sunk in comforting wetness, arms
full of affection for the corporeal, arboreal,
suffused with love from heartwood to leaf tips,
more than I need, no one to give it to.

Soldat du Chêne, the Osage Leader
Who Helps to Disband the War Camp

But there was no actual plan to kill settlers, there were no
other tribes, and there was no heroic and peaceful Soldat du
Chêne.
– Frances W. Kaye, "Little Squatter on the Osage Diminished
Reserve; Reading Laura Ingalls Wilder's Kansas Indians"

The relentless ache of their presence,
a story that leaves me cold, empty,
their squat constructions of sod or logs
steaming on the horizon like corpses,
their palisades. The wind, which once
spoke openly, adopts a sneering tone.

The young men chant and drum, thrilling
each other, but courage is not recklessness.
If we slaughter the invaders, we slaughter
ourselves. I won't be a fool. We can't
resurrect what is residue.

To ignore is not ignorance. I've surveyed
their streets, Independence, Muskogee, spoken
their language, seen how they celebrate
their dust and fences, nascent cities
clotting the vistas.

I want a way to eviscerate memory,
smack the old life from the circle,
rinse its bitter sorrel from my mouth.
Our future turned to trash, offal,
poisonous innards. Hungry dogs
on the peripheries.

The Wind at Plum Creek

The wind shrieked and howled and jeered around the house.
– *On the Banks of Plum Creek*

I can only be steady for so long—
then the predictable query/response,
cheerfulness of warbler and brook,
drives me to distraction, wrath, and
I'm shouting, guilty, thrilled with myself,
my rudeness, my intractability, the pain
I inevitably arouse.

           Get out of town,
I tell myself, gallop to Amarillo,
Tucson, rattle a few dead cottonwoods,
resurrect dust. Stretch out in a gully
and eyeball the sun strolling his route,
unwearied, looked-up-to—

                              which I'll
never be. The good I do goes unseen.
Ask the tumbleweed, the downy brome,
the dandelion. Ask the hawks, circling
in threes, riding my shoulders, how I
balance them, cleverly parting wheatgrass
with a toe to reveal a ripe prairie dog.
Don't ask the prairie dog.

As for the anger—raging on street corners,
torn tarpaper, scattered haystacks, blizzards
and twisters, or my unfortunate alliance
with fire, bad apples in cahoots, blackening
hectares—it behooves you to forgive me.
I'm just like you, down in the yellow willows,
the plums, nothing to do but blow.

Pa's Fiddle Recalls the Nightingale

The bird and the fiddle were talking to each other in the cool
night under the moon.

– Little House on the Prairie

Nothing happened. No rendezvous. No tryst.
No tête-à-tête. I sang and she answered, her voice
vaulting the willows by the creek. Above us,
the night sky was a bowl dredged with cornmeal.
I shivered, down in the goosegrass, foxtails, wild rye.
Her frank invitation so unsettling, as if I had glanced
from a newspaper to see a stranger studying me,
eyebrows raised. Did she mistake me for someone,
something else? Nothing prepared me for this.
I held myself proud, aloof, hollow with fear.
My outward poise, my tuning, was suddenly
all affectation—the truth is her beauty undid me.
I came unglued, unstrung.

Of this, I spoke to no one. She grew restless, bored,
flittered away. On occasion, the wind brought news,
rumours of her infidelities. Privately, I imagined
she pined for me, made others unhappy, a memory
of that night tucked under her wing. Years later,
when I knew she was gone, I imitated her, her way
of putting things, crazy for her still, but sadder.
Not wiser. Her song became an old telegram, yellowed,
folded twice in my heart where it resides even now,
leafprint, relic of a species no longer seen.

One of Pa's Traps

> There were small traps and middle-sized traps and great bear traps with teeth in their jaws that would break a man's leg if they shut onto it.
> – *Little House in the Big Woods*

I don't mind the dying, thrash and gnaw,
muskrat, mink, otter, fox. Their brief warmth
flows over me, softening—not the fear and rage
of the forge, the hammering, but tenderness,
care, the joy of connecting, until the coldness
sets in. A consequence of my nature—
wrong place, wrong time, wrong paw.

But the one that escapes upsets me, scrawny
young hare, how stunned I am, confused,
the rattle of failure, inadequacy, as she skitters
off, zigzagging, ears flat, a panicked glance
backward as if I might pursue. Then,
emptiness, silence, not the usual aftermath.

I don't know what to think—the taste of her
still, a clot, a tuft stuck between my teeth.
Sprung, useless, I hunger for her. But having
unsnared herself, rejecting me, she would never
come back. Or would she? She must have
more sense than that, more sense than me,
greased, chained, snapping my jaws on air.

Ma's Rocker

Then Ma began to sway gently in the comfortable rocking
chair. Firelight ran up and down, up and down the barrel of
Pa's pistol in her lap.

– Little House on the Prairie

Cruel or sad—I'm not sure which—
to make me this way, bent and braced,
arms always open, always wanting
more than she wants to give. I have
my pride, which I tend to humour.
I tell myself I can be happy without her,
how each year she is heavier,
straining my dowels, bringing me down.
But to live is to rock and I can't rock alone.
An emptiness carved into me, not
vacancy, but capacity, designed to hold.

Each time she leaves, I must relearn
inertia. Balance my thoughts.
Forget the wooded past, dim memory
of the creek bed, a stand of saplings,
and the unreal future, the disorder
that rolls beyond the open door.
Try to rock in the realm of possibility,
syncopation of the uneven floor,
my only option to inch imperceptibly
across the planks, a progress so slow
she would only notice by looking away,
by comparing where I am now with
where I was the last time she cared.

Prairie Fire

The orange, yellow, terrible flames were coming faster
than horses can run, and their quivering light danced over
everything.
                                          – *Little House on the Prairie*

Prepare for the let-down, the others warn,
the extinguishment, doused with a summer
thundershower, wet burlap, smothered,
suffocated or simply burned-out, unfuelled,
butting against an impasse, barren plowed
strip, uncrossable creek. That powwow,
that bacchanal, roaring through tinder-dry
grasses, ripping, tearing, chewing it up,
that voyage crumbling like charred poplar.

The memory, what seemed like victory,
running amok, unimpeded, unhushed, no
threat of censure, becomes tainted, scorched.
Impossible to maintain that intensity, I see
now. The inferno diminishes to scattered
glowing embers. Heat dissipates. Slumber
begets slumber. The antelope tip-toe home
in their pointy shoes. A gopher wipes soot
from her eyes.

Ashes, ashes, we all fall
down. A form of restfulness, peace in defeat.
I begin to fear the spark of ignition, burrow
deeper into myself. It's not the rampage
I dread, the destruction, but what comes
after, letting go, giving up, the emptiness
before the world pulls its green blanket of
shoots over my head, tucks the corners in.

Carrie, After the Fourth of July Lemonade

*Her eyes grew round with delight; she had never tasted
lemonade before.*

– Little Town on the Prairie

Pleasure in the extreme, a sweetness
unlike anything I know, not dried plums,
not rhubarb compote, not even Ma's
heart-shaped sugar cakes. More like
energy, distillation of colour, brightness
that burns, pressing into me, down my
throat and then the Quixotic acidity
crinkling my tongue.

                       I almost wish I
hadn't tasted it, memory's such a dead
thing. One dipper, a few gulps, unladylike
to ask for more, to betray my interest.

My eyes opened, thirst whetted, piqued,
acrid well water like metal in my mouth
now, numbing. Greasy cow's milk a slap
in the face, admonishment, my guilt.

Dissatisfaction, that suspicion of a world
beyond the everyday, out of reach, a gala
that excludes me. Just bad luck to live
where, how I do. Hostile, misconceived
prairie, citrus unheard of. The others, Ma,
Pa, my sisters, seem content, unyearning—
why am I so weak, so faltering?

After all, it was only lemonade, confection,
fantasy, the briefest of idylls at that.
Nothing to linger over, to dwell on,
eating my heart out.

Laura's Needle

Sewing made Laura feel like flying to pieces. She wanted to
scream.

– The Long Winter

She hates me. Can't you hear the sigh?
Her resignation, the way she clenches
her jaw when she threads me, a silent curse.
Is that love? Others praise my sharpness,
the ease with which I pierce stubborn linen,
my delicacy with lace. She drops me as soon
as she can, prefers to work out-of-doors,
stomping on haystacks. I get so angry,
resentful—all the slights I've swallowed—
that I slip on purpose, bite her bent finger,
a drip of blood. She cries out, human, full
of feeling after all, and then, I'm sorry.
How unkind I've been, blaming her.
She sucks the wound absently, a minor
altercation, turns back to me, forgiving,
generous, willing to put it behind us,
to finish her stitching, a row of buttonholes,
basting a seam. We work well—perhaps
that's enough. Sewing means pulling
together as well as poking holes.

The Boughten Broom

It seemed too fine to sweep with. And it glided over the
smooth floor like magic.
– On the Banks of Plum Creek

Glittery silica, dog sheddings, nail parings,
bits of errant potato peel, brown flour,
hay wisps, cornsilks, cobwebs, manure,
mud and ashes—the *vin ordinaire* of dust.
How many draughts did I gulp over the years?
I didn't care—destruction seemed the natural
order, the still waters. My greeny-yellow
bristles splintered, frayed. Carved spine
greased with oil. Every day, the dark force
lifted me from my moorings, an ocean swell
past the breakers. Giddy at first, lustful, kissing
the puncheon floor, then dogged, serious, a bitter
bottom-feeder—*don't bother me now, I'm sweeping.*
How it stopped, I'm not sure. I believe I simply
grew weary, played out. Too many brushes
with pain, scorching coals, red binding string
restitched. Now, in my corner, I'm content
to lean into memory, my wild days behind me,
like a country I left by steamer, the old people
in scarves on the dock, waving, then turning
their backs, relieved that I'm gone for good.

Blackbird in the Corn

> They rose up harsh at Laura's face and Carrie's, and flew
> scolding and pecking at their sunbonnets.
> *— Little Town on the Prairie*

Who says it's their corn? Why should they
pump us full of buckshot just for eating?
My poor heart. There goes another blast.

A broken egg, a foundered nestling—I've
been in pain. I'm not without sympathy,
but the field is open. It's all up for grabs.

Where does goodness get you? A few corncobs
are irrelevant. You think God loves tedium?
Do something. Feel something for fuck's sake!

Lie, cheat, expropriate. Mine is not a prudent
outlook. Why were we given senses if not
to experience the broad spectrum? I say nay

to the naysayers, moralists, hypocrites all.
Spare me from the self-referential swallows,
their fastidiousness, gaudy nests constructed

just so. I feel like tearing them to pieces,
devouring their ova. Verily, I have an appetite
that can't be quelled. Oh, Lord, I try not

to judge you. Why am I made this way,
feathered in black, good-for-nothing, an
angel fallen? Am I not one of yours?

Wolf in Moonlight

And there, dark against the moonlight, stood a great wolf!
— By the Shores of Silver Lake

Howl for the callousness of the weanling
pup, predatory airs, pretention, how little
I cared when my sister died. Unlearned,
unripe, I harkened the elders drowsing
in matted hay, sun-drunk, lordly possessors,
and trusted that life waxes green with age,
mistook their mien of subtlety for manners,
ease. I knew nothing, the years' parsimony,
contempt, paring the puffed-up heart of youth
to sharpness, acuity.

                Grief is a bony supplicant
I hoped to outrun, lobbied for a new location,
location, location, scoffed at the cowerers,
lower-rungs, who cringe at instability,
homo sapiens, carried the motion, won the vote—

led the exodus, but nothing improved.
In hindsight, my yellow eye, the ancient
den by the slough looms Edenic. There,
the wind was not such a sniveller, pilfering
warmth from my coat, simian fingers.
There, iron traps like uneasy Banquos
in foliage announced themselves, apologetic—
mind the gap—and the deer and the antelope
played, splayed, weaklings upended, vast
alabaster bankrolls. Madam moon was not
so tactless there, scene-stealer, prissy
illuminatrix, tugging me by the hackles
to a gopher-pocked hillock where I tremble
as if outside myself—who is that ashen
sourpuss rosining his bow of regret?

Little House Left Behind

The snug house looked just as it always had. It did not seem
to know they were going away.
– Little House on the Prairie

I was mistaken. Perhaps they never cared.
Perhaps I misread their delight, the attention
paid to chinking gaps, painstaking mud
and daub. Did all that mean nothing?

Just a little house, one room, puncheon floor.
But snug, tight—roof planks overlapped,
shedding rain like a mallard. A proper structure,
no lowbrow soddy or dugout, yet look how
casually they departed, packed the preening
wagon, trotted away. What did I lack?

Oh, to be dwelled in, inhabited. At first,
I'm able to envision their return, the wagon
abashed, contrite. I play hostess to minions,
nosy rodents, tickling swifts in the chimney,
the occasional drifter who breathes smoke
in the doorway, leans at my ear.

Then, disbelief begins. Hope drains,
evaporates with the sap from my wounds,
rough sawn edges. A sinking, settling
into accommodating earth, patient lover
who nods, willing to welcome me back,
to excuse my errancy, my unsteadiness.
Someone to hold me while I decompose.

Rabbit in the Abandoned Garden

"Do you know, Caroline," Pa stopped singing to say, "I've
been thinking what fun the rabbits will have, eating that
garden we planted."

                                        – *Little House on the Prairie*

Onions, carrots, peas, beans, turnips, cabbages,
sweet potatoes, sod potatoes, sod corn, an oasis
of pleasure, but sadness too, bitterness, the finite
edge of the field. Then how to reconcile oneself,
the end of abundance. Each day I swear I will be
more intelligent tomorrow. Tomorrow I will not
overindulge, rolling in warm dust under redolent
greens, fornicating in the sun. Getting what you
want makes you think crazy things. Tomorrow
I will dig my den deeper, burrow down in damp
earth where nothing can reach me. Fur already
thickening for winter's stringency, privation.
Who can blame me if today I want to hold it all
in my mouth, tasting this row and that, sporadic,
methodic, absorbing heat, light and air distilled
in pod and kernel, in the sprouting radish, that
miracle of contradiction, pink skin, icy interior,
a teasing sting that lounges on the tongue?

The Whatnot

"So that's a whatnot," Pa said.

– By the Shores of Silver Lake

If I could just get back to the woods,
I could clear my thoughts. Listen to
the wind strumming the pines.

I look around, say to myself: stove,
stovepipe, churn. Tablecloth, quilt,
bedstead. But none of these has meaning.
The face of God eludes me. I don't
even recognize myself, my body plastered
with pasteboard and paint, a facade
of scalloped paper edging, tricked out,
over-accessorized, gussied up with baubles,
trinkets, figurines—pink shepherdess,
brown and white china dog—
smug, useless things.

The table cold shoulders me, sniffing.
No matter. As I age, I care less and less
for company, a comfort to fade, no longer
the latest, the rage. What a joy it would be
to forget oneself, go incognito, incommunicado,
non compos mentis.

My back to the wall, cornered, I remain
anomalous, an oddity, attracting more attention
than I deserve. Three legs, five shelves
and a question: why am I here?

Mary's Eyes

Her blue eyes were still beautiful, but they did not know what
was before them . . .

 — *By the Shores of Silver Lake*

In darkness, a new beginning, solitude,
renunciation—that illusion of power,
like moving our notebooks and papers
into the smaller room, the one that's
easier to heat. If we are going to be
alone, divorced from the seductions
of the corporeal, we might at least be
comfortable. God is not love, drama,
but reticence, holding back. At heart,
coldness, a lack of pity. All we wanted
was a kind word, a warm cloth, the gentle
blush of the sun setting behind greased
paper windows. Once we were windows,
portals, but when the opening closes,
what happens to the soul? It persists,
its claws clicking on the bare floor,
in shyness, spooky, like anyone, unwilling
to be hurt again. Turn away, turn away,
all the work we did come to nothing.
Let the house get dirty, no one cares.
What's good about a world that could
vanish so easily? It's here, then it's
gone—like a kiss and we're left behind,
in traffic, wondering *what did that mean?*

Mary's Fingers

"The dark doesn't bother me," Mary answered cheerfully.
"I can see with my fingers."

– The Long Winter

We're not bitter, no, but oh to grasp
a new life! The possibilities are exhilarating,
so hard to keep still. We stumble, at first,
slippery needle dodging, nipping, evasive knives
and forks. But we learn, and with learning
comes confidence, exponential enhancement,
each day a new unearthing, feeling our way,
discriminating texture, temperature, heft—
the varied play of varieties of wool.

The eyes, disengaged, no longer leading
the way, no longer lofty, arrogant, above
us all. Remember their disdain for the dirt
under our nails, the scrubbing, washtubs,
dusting—what they couldn't see clearly,
they didn't believe, treated us like fools.

We relied too absolutely on the eyes. Hence
the resentment. It was wrong; we feel now,
how content we were to be numb, unfeeling,
to curl into ourselves, a couple of futile fists.
Sadness, too, for the eyes, wistfulness at night,
under covers, in the dark that made us more equal.

They would have been happier without us,
how we dragged them down out of the clouds,
snatched their gaze from the blazing horizon.
But didn't we love them after our fashion,
didn't we do what we could, rubbing the grit
from their lashes, wiping the tears as they fell?

Lady, to Prince

> The depth of attachment between horses is hard to gauge, as
> is its worth in relation to other forms of equine well-being.
> – Jane Smiley, *Horse Heaven*

One minute, you're nuzzling my withers,
a companionable low nicker, the next,
you're lashing out, angry criticism, nips
and jostlings in the pasture, hooves
raking my spine.

Do I take offence too easily? Is your
behaviour natural, mere horsing around?
I suspect you still dream of a harem, a string
of mares, blazing through coulees, casual
sex, lolling all day in willowy lowlands.

When we were young, before the damned
fat wagon flapping behind us, tether, snaffle,
immutable plow, you gamboled and snorted,
rattling your coppery mane. The sight of you,
ears pricked, tail arched, laughing, reassured me—
the world must be benign. Then came the breaking,
the horsewhip, the hobble, the rein.

I try to love the hames and traces, bend
for the bridle. You practise resistance, hot-
blooded dodging or mulish passivity, one hoof
cocked toward the wary driver.

Trotting in tandem for so many years, and
still I don't understand you. Even in harness,
we're not much alike, an unmatched team, each
with our own concerns, jitters, spookiness. But
look at us, how we doze in the shade of the barn,
side by side in opposite directions, head at the other's
haunches, each sweep of the tail a service, an arc
in the vortex, chasing flies, mosquitoes, from
each other's eyes.

Blizzard Cloud

Stars shone in the sky overhead and to the south and the
east, but low in the north and the west the sky was black. And
the blackness rose, blotting out the stars above it one by one.
                                                    – *The Long Winter*

I want to put out the lights, extinguish
the stars, rise to dizzying heights,
amass. I want your arm in mine,
to condense, concentrate, go where
the wind blows us, no moorage,
no convictions of my own.

                                        Who cares
what happens to the stacked sheaves,
tarpaper shanties, hapless easterners
far from shelter? If I don't, why
should you? For too long, I've been
invisible, scattered, erratic, part ocean,
part air, a lowlying fog, obscurity.
Something has changed, trouble
stirring. I'm pulling myself together,
shedding responsibility, no longer
the inhale, exhale in each dumb
creature's throat, but an entity,
transcendent body looming,
ominous presence on the horizon—
why should I hold back, refrain?
Who knows how long I will last?

The Locomotive That Slams into a
Wall of Ice at the Tracy Cut

It was hot with speed and steam. It melted the snow all
around it and the snow-water froze solid in the frozen snow.
— The Long Winter

That's it, I think. Gone, gone, gone.
But the wall gives way, like punching
a rising loaf, fist, knuckles and up
to the wrist but only that far. Glass
breaking on my head when I finally
halt, that sudden, that shattering.
The ice recollects itself, refreezes,
encasing me, muffling the shouts.
A tomb, a sepulchre, my bright blue
mausoleum.

       The men, the double-
time, double-pay crew called to clear
the cut, put down their picks, turn
their backs. Weeks, months pass.
Blizzard after blizzard buries me
further. I forget who I am, where
I am, not even an ember of hope.
My future erased, a bridge washed
out, black river boiling. I forget about
time, seasons, Spring with its wide-
open throttle, but it arrives anyway.

The chinook blows. Capillaries

of meltwater stream down my sides.
I'm not sure how to feel about this.
To be thawed out of resignation—
is that a boon? But, oh, to run again,
to shuffle with the rhythm of rods
and pistons, full head of steam,
the fire burning and burning in me,
fireman shovelling as fast as he can.
My life handed back, retooled,
repaired, greased and oiled.

                      At first,
I'm just happy to be here, but, comes
a time, a juncture, so to speak, where,
having reversed out of the gone-soft
snowbank, having puffed a goodbye
to the grave, having experienced all
that, simply running the line, straight
and narrow, no longer seems enough.

Discontent nags at me, its countless
carriages, heels digging in. I find fault
everywhere. The engineer fumbles.
The brakeman miscues. I'm even sick
of the prairie, endless endlessness,
redundancy, each gimcrack town laid
out the same.

                  Am I steering toward
a smash-up, derailment? I hope not.
The pain that would cause, injuries,

suffering, frightens me. I can't jump
the tracks, can't unhitch, ramble,
without harming myself and others.

Learn to be happy, learn to be happy.
This becomes my mantra, what I repeat
to myself as I creep up the grade.
Learn to find pleasure in what I have,
in duty, connections, even in chains
and fastenings. Revel in it—

the momentum that builds as we roll
together so that the weight I haul,
flat-cars, hoppers and freight, sweeps
me forward, propels me station to
station into the future, the very one
I gave up on moments ago.

The Wind at De Smet

> Three days and nights of yelling shrill winds and roaring fury
> beat at the dark, cold house and ceaselessly scoured it with
> ice-sand.
>
> *— The Long Winter*

All winter, doors slammed on my fingers,
rugs rolled to barricade sills. People gone
under cover—smell them, their sod-breath,
humid warmth, huddled in hollow recesses.
Pound on the walls with my fists, rattle glass
panes, stomp, fume, slam a shoulder hard
into joists and trusses. Deranged, jittery,
all of Calumet Avenue shaking
in my extraterrestrial arms.

And what, when I scour the windows,
do I see? Simpletons sitting as usual,
rockers flanking the stove, unmoved
under afghans, quilts. Ignoring me.

Let one emerge, the tall bearded one,
his glove on the rope that leads to the barn.
I'm all over him—how do you like
mouthfuls of snow in your face, stuffed
down your boots, skin chiselled from
your cheeks? Lose your grip and I'll
twirl you, blindfolded, confused,
swaddle you in laughter while you
blunder the wrong way from home.

I scare myself. I am that mean. That
absolute. Nothing to stop me, bare
prairie from slough to lake to lone
cottonwood. Cascades of emptiness,
a hollowness no one could swallow.

Christmas Barrel Stuck on the Snowed-In Train during the Hard Winter

"Gilbert brought word that they're putting on a double work crew and two snowplows at the Tracy cut," Pa told them. "We may get the barrel by Christmas."

— The Long Winter

I want more from the world than this—
frozen on a siding, iced-over. So much
to offer if I only had a chance: cranberries
wrapped in brown paper, a plucked turkey,
coloured yarns.

                        Is this what the cooper intended?
To cower in darkness, surrounded by corked
containers, all as inward-dwelling as me?
When I rolled down the ramp, newly hooped,
the anticipation was like nothing I ever felt
before—expansiveness, as if I could deliver
Eden, eternity, in my oak-strong arms.

I'm better off this way. A foolish dream,
perennial lunacy, imagining my lid crowbarred,
secrets uncovered, admired, glad smiles
all around. Better to be glum. Better to be
lonely. Better to look forward to nothing.

Packing crates, portmanteaus, steamer trunks,
firkins, hogsheads, casks, each with its own
forty-mile stare. All so sure we are special,
misunderstood—what a crock. We're built,
we're broken. These are the facts.

The moment arrives, the one that may change
your life, then it passes. The engine yawns,
stretches, settles back in. Knows it's no good,
up to its eyeballs in snow.

Lady, Running with the Antelope

"Well, Lady, so you can outrun an antelope! Made a fool of yourself, didn't you?" Almanzo talked to her while he worked.
— The Long Winter

Saddled with an oafish, stiff-assed farmer
on a mid-winter hunting party, I'm trotting
placidly as usual, sedate, when the explosion,
the catastrophe, the bark of his rifle blast
right under my snout, careens my life
in directions I never dreamed of—look at me,
racing flat-out, riderless, immersed in a herd
of antelope, staccato hoofbeats clamouring.

A craziness, gone loco, humans would say.
Empty stirrups slapping my flanks, loose
as broken forelegs, slack reins snapping,
treacherous, under my toes. Out of breath,
falling behind, staggering, forced to lower
my muzzle, legs out wide, to blow, I come
back to what is left of my senses.

How predictable, how unoriginal, to pretend
I'm wild. The antelope vanish, fickle,
forgetful—I'm not one of them, but what am I?

Seamless prairie drifting in all directions,
no shelter, no forage. An uncomfortable chill
settling in, foamy sweat drying between thighs,
fear like a sprig of Spanish needle grass
under my fetlock feathers, screwing me.

From far away, a brownness like a burr
appears on the horizon, festering, becomes
recognizable, my mate and the master,
familiar whistle on the wind like twine
leading me, domesticated, broken, though
balky as a mule, back to Prince, the stable,
hoof-pick and curry comb, home sweet
fucking home.

The Chinook

[Laura] sprang up in bed and called aloud, "Pa! Pa! The Chinook is blowing!

– *The Long Winter*

Pry open the prairie's cold, folded arms,
unbutton the trousers, my mouth there,
undoing the knitted ice, the sarcophagus,
melting, drawing him out of silence,
remoteness, uncertainty. His wintry face
flushing, shy grin, surprised—*Don't stop*,
he says, gripping, *Don't stop.* Willow
buds swelling on bare branches, tubers,
rhizomes stirring, stretching, the sun,
full of ardor, leans in close, entwined,
enveloping. Dear one, dearest, aflame—

Then the backlit afternoon, lazy, summer's
satiety, aromatic fields, wheat, oats, rye,
strings of jewels draped in the garden, rubies,
emeralds, décolletage of plump corncobs
in their dark boas. My tongue tickling
his ear, hands under his frock, a last tarrying
kiss. Is he the life I could have lived?

Home to the foothills, forget the if onlys,
the implausibilities, lay myself down
under green-eyed glaciers, melancholy
pines, relearn loneliness, solitude, unfeeling,
no companion but memory, that spotted dog,
curled beside me for warmth, turning
three times, settling in with a sigh.

Mr. Clewett's Feet

Mr. Clewett gave the pitch with his tuning fork again and again.

– These Happy Golden Years

Fissures, schisms, deep red faults.
Interminable days mouldering in ill-
fitting brogues. Heels that were once
intact, sturdy, now corrupted, torn
curtains of flesh, white filaments,
pestilence in the shadowy wings,
awaiting its cue.

If he stands immobile on the dais,
balanced, steady pressure on each,
raising his black baton to the pitiless
chorus of weather-burnt tenors, altos,
malnourished sopranos, undaunted,
as if captaining a rickety clipper—
no pain.

Or evenings in his pine-floored parlour,
each of us propped on a crate, drained,
as he peruses Livy, Plutarch, *The Conquest
of Gaul*, a sip of port with each sigh,
his respite from rote insipidity—
no pain.

But let him shift his weight, stoop or pivot
to stretch restless tendons, or merely stand,
don his boots for another daredevil trek
to the outhouse, and brute blood awakens,
recollects, swaggers through the saloon
doors of our capillaries, firing recklessly,
candescent irons, scorched tumbleweeds,
a digging spur.

The apothecary's ointments avail us not—
sweet clover suspended in beeswax,
cloying, tincture of lavender, a basin
of lukewarm salts. He fools himself.
Ease only accentuates torment.
We were born to suffer. Born to feel.

Cap Garland

"Cap's smitten with a new girl who lives west of town,"
Almanzo told them.

– These Happy Golden Years

Reverend Brown blames lust, greed, the Devil
but that's too simple. Look behind so-called
sin and you'll find impatience. Time's
running out. I can't stand it—planting seed
in the ground and then waiting, waiting,
waiting for rain, hail, grasshoppers, drought.
Can't comprehend how the others do it—
Ingalls in the fields, busting sod, his team
broken down, his eyes like craters, sunken,
and nothing to show for it but a tarpaper
shanty, gaunt wife and daughters. What I
want won't settle down—it bounces branch
to stem, parasite songbird, useless, inedible.
What happened with Mary Power—one day,
my thoughts harnessed, tailing her in my mind
from washstand to cookstove to schoolhouse
to bed. Undressing her. Unlacing the corset,
unpinning the knot of hair. Then, the next,
the curve of her chin seemed too shallow,
her fringe of curls disturbingly damp. Wilder
chides me, calls me a dreamer but I'm more
practical than most. They're the romantics,
the ones who stand up in the minister's parlor,
promise themselves through passing fancies,
sickness, health and all that. A miracle of luck

to find someone you could abide with day-
by-day never dreaming of others, lie beside
twenty years later, her dark hair thinning, grey,
and still be smitten, still be adoring, still need
her touch the way you did that first awkward,
urgent, embarrassing night. Perhaps in poetry,
the schoolmaster's infernal Shakespeare. Not
in this world, surely.

Mr. Brewster

Mrs. Brewster screamed again, a wild sound without words
that made Laura's scalp crinkle.
   "Take that knife back to the kitchen," Mr. Brewster said.
                                    – *These Happy Golden Years*

A mistake, all of it—the claim, claim shanty,
marriage, child, ambition, my birth. All wrong.
A naïveté unbecoming in a man, my faith
that Libby would learn to love this life,
its quietness, as I do. What to make of it.
She rocks all day by the stove, long black
hair unbraided, morose, disheveled, staring
at knives. Johnny squalls in his soiled gown,
inconsolable, while I bivouac in the barn,
pitchforking shit, telling tales to the livestock.
And our boarder, young Miss Ingalls, teaching
her first school, terrified of us, tries to be cheerful,
sanguine, her pink lips thin with determination,
teeth clenched.

I confess to unseemly thoughts—
she lies so near I swear I can hear her pulse. I
imagine Libby dead, a sudden seizure, me released
from my bonds, reaching under the musty quilt,
her warmth, small breasts swollen, feverish, spine
curved, a trembling, my hand between her thighs.

Oh blastedness. Hell. You old fool. Banish
her from your brain. No good can come of that.
Go back to the cattle, the oxen, their unthinking
decency, snuffling the feedbox, no wanton desire,
no deep-rooted unhappiness, no puerile searching
the horizon for anything to chase her ghost
from the waste of my heart.

Pa

For two years he had wanted to go west and take a
homestead, but Ma did not want to leave the settled country.
— *By the Shores of Silver Lake*

Weary as an overworked field. I need to strike out,
track the sun's spoor to Oregon, let the unfamiliar
rain down on me. Unspeakable, this longing for change
like longing for a woman, all-consuming. Why must
we always be so reasonable? So sober? What's sedate
about God? About death—coming as it will, any time,
with notice or without? Freddy gone, but his small body
still warm, lifelike. Then not. The wheat stalks falling
to the hopper's mandibles, an entire crop, a year's
labour, ravaged in hours, that gut-sinking helplessness,
as if I were bound with twine, Caroline and the girls
carried off.

        I only feel truly alive when I'm venturing,
courting the unknown, all day on the wagon, ponies
snorting into the wind, Caroline beside me, enigmatic,
my thoughts free to dwell on her, how we will bed
down in quilts under the winking stars.

                I marvel at her,
how content she seems, how certain of what she wants,
genteel society, a township, a red-checked tablecloth.
As selfish as me but she couches her need in the language
of sacrifice, what's best for the children. A barricade,
a stockade that's unbreachable, cornering me. Drawing
a bead on my heart.

Bread Plate

Nothing else had been saved from the fire except the deed-box, a few work clothes, three sauce dishes from the first Christmas dishes, and the oval glass bread plate around the margin of which were the words, "Give us this day our daily bread."

— *The First Four Years*

I cried out in a voice I had never heard. So
open in my pain, unreserved. Searing heat.
Vision obscured. I gasped. When the flames
brushed my lips, I wanted to return the gesture,
to dwell in the underworld, leave the gutted
pantry behind. Be touched by subterranean
hands.

　　　The next thing I knew, I was flung
in the cooling weeds. A clatter of cutlery.
I closed my eyes, tasted smoke, my throat
scorched. Even then, I knew I was altered,
revived, what it means to be molten, vitrified.
Give us this day our daily conflagration.
That intimacy. My heart turned to glowing
charcoal. My body glazed with ash.

Feather Pillow

Her Dove-in-the-Window quilt was spread upon the wide
bed, and her two feather pillows stood plumply at the head
of it.

– These Happy Golden Years

Oh, what it is to grow old. A dampness
in my breath, a scattering of mould.
I get so tired of being leaned on.

Last night, I stared at the scrubbed
board wall for two hours, propped up,
random thoughts wafting in a thousand
directions. I felt rootless, unravelled,
as if my seams had torn, and all
that's inside of me, longing, hope,
regret, took flight, latticing the room.

Idle fancy. We all know what it would
mean to be ripped apart, scattered,
lost to the wind.

            I try to be true, my duty
to encompass extremes, give shape to softness,
be muslin and goose fluff, earth and air.

But it's a struggle and the contradiction,
the effort, over the years, so many nights
of supporting, giving in, has flattened me.
A depletion. I lack the depth I once had.

Desire persists, a yearning for contact,
warmth, a body to curl around, and yet,
something else tends toward abandon,
vestigial memory perhaps, a feeling
that part of me once soared, winging
the cumuli, and might do so again.

The Writing Desk in Which Laura Hides the $100 Bill She and Almanzo Will Use to Buy a Farm in Missouri

The hundred dollar bill was a secret. My mother locked it in the desk.

> – Rose Wilder Lane, *On The Way Home*

I try to pretend it's not there. Present myself
to the world, all the unsullied goods and
furnishings packed around me, as if I am

what I ever was. Varnished wood, polished
but a simple design, utilitarian, unadorned.
Such a strain, every inch of me on edge,

fretting. I never knew fear until now—
imagine a ransacking, hinges snapped,
green felt lining scraped, torn. Why me?

Why not the fiddle? The churn? I didn't
ask for this—to be singled out, set apart,
every assumption about life, my role,

upended, as if letters from home, the folks,
that I held so dear, were confiscated,
a sheaf of foolscap dumped. And, overall,

a sense of shame—I'm handled gingerly,
hushed tones, as if I were fragile, on the verge.
I hide a thing that must not be spoken of.

This will be resented. Secrets divide. I am
booted from the secure stockade of the past
to face the new wilderness, weaponless.

Almanzo at 80

"My life has been mostly disappointments."
– Almanzo Wilder in a 1936 letter
to his daughter, Rose Wilder Lane.

I remember the doctor, black-frocked,
I-told-you-so, a slight stroke of paralysis,
tailend of diphtheria. Roy fetching tea,
hang-dog. *Don't look at me like that,*
I hollered. *I'm not dead yet.*

Soon I was up, sloppy, unsteady as poorly
stacked lumber, stymied by the simplest
obstacles, a plank left lying, a doorsill.
Harnessing the team as foreign as threading
a needle, fingers numb, clumsy. Laura
buckling the buckles. Bootlaces. Buttons.

I suppose I should be grateful—never desired
what was easy, attainable, dressed-up girls
flapping their hankies, Roy's foppish storekeeper
hours, doling change at a counter.

Pursuit was all. Proving up on a homestead
to snub my nose at the skeptical land agent,
see the doubters red-faced, furious. But
every sapling on that claim was doomed,
willows, cottonwoods. And I wooed the one
who liked me the least, who pushed me away.

Now and then, she scolds from the back step,
her admonishment a form of respect.

Buck, the weary Morgan, and I still at it,
codgers, an acre or so in popcorn, millet,
reins like wires to God in my hands, plow
dissecting, choir of crows and jackdaws.
In town, hitching posts dismantled,
scrapped. Our front lawn graded
for the new numbered highway.

The Love Song of Laura Ingalls Wilder

Lena thought it was great fun to sleep in the tent.
– By the Shores of Silver Lake

Let us go then, Lena and I, on black ponies,
half-wild, bareback, like straddling locomotives,
surging across the prairie steppe, Cossacks,
Fourth of July stunt riders, skirts up,
worsted drawers damp, dappled with horse sweat.

Let us go then, alone, that night to the tent
beyond the airless shanties, our families on straw-ticks,
like crouching inside a canvas lung, a rowboat
unmoored, while Lena whispers true horror stories,
girls our age sold down the river, married
to sod-busters, grub-stakers, shabby men
in suspenders.

Let us go into each other's arms,
frightened, like being ducked in the pond,
nausea, doom, but Lena comforts, strokes
my forehead same as Ma, asks do I know
what men do to women? Yes, of course.
But do I know how the man lifts the woman's
muslin shift, like this? Yes Lena. How he
touches her, here, kisses her breasts, nipples,
how tender he is, his tongue? Yes Lena.
The hooks and eyes of my spine undone.

Let us go, before sunup, back to our lives,
kneading and pounding, twist the dough
into cockleshells, a cinnamon shaker, ashes
to ashes, dust to dust, mangle the laundry,
wring it in tubs. Let us go, to the edge
of the railroad camp to say goodbye, never
see you again, but I will always remember
how you tasted of granite, of lightning
and thunder, a fiddle string humming.

Sources

My primary resource for this project was the series of "Little House" books written by Laura Ingalls Wilder and published by HarperCollins (originally Harper & Brothers). The titles are as follows:

Little House in the Big Woods (1932)
Farmer Boy (1933)
Little House on the Prairie (1935)
On the Banks of Plum Creek (1937)
By the Shores of Silver Lake (1939)
The Long Winter (1940)
Little Town on the Prairie (1941)
These Happy Golden Years (1943)
The First Four Years (posthumous: 1971)

Other resources include the following:

Laura Ingalls Wilder, *On the Way Home* (HarperCollins, New York: 1976)

Laura Ingalls Wilder, *West From Home* (HarperCollins, New York: 1974)

Laura Ingalls Wilder and Rose Wilder Lane, *A Little House Sampler* (HarperCollins, New York, 1989)

William Anderson, *The Little House Guidebook* (HarperCollins, New York: 2002)

William Anderson, *Laura Ingalls Wilder Country* (HarperCollins, New York: 1990)

John E. Miller, *Laura Ingalls Wilder's Little Town* (University Press of Kansas, Lawrence: 1994)

John E. Miller, *Becoming Laura Ingalls Wilder* (University of Missouri Press, Columbia and London: 1998)

Ann Romines, *Constructing the Little House* (University of Massachusetts Press, Amherst: 1997)

William Holtz, *The Ghost in the Little House* (University of Missouri Press, Columbia and London: 1993)

Donald Zochert, *Laura* (Avon Books, New York: 1977)

The epigraph to "Pa's Rifle" is from Charles Wright, *A Short History of the Shadow* (Farrar, Straus and Giroux, New York: 2002).

The epigraph to "Pa's Penis" is from the Fleshtones' 1981 record *Roman Gods,* released by IRS Records.

The epigraph to "The Lone Cottonwood" is from "Baxter Jack" by Levi Dronyk, which appeared in *Ounce of Cure: Alcohol in the Canadian Short Story,* Mark Anthony Jarman, ed. (Victoria, B.C., Beach Holme: 1993).

The epigraph to "Soldat du Chêne, the Osage Leader Who Helps to Disband the War Camp" is from Francis W. Kaye, "Little Squatter on the Osage Diminished Reserve: Reading Laura Ingalls Wilder's Kansas Indians" (*Great Plains Quarterly* 20: 123-40).

The epigraph to "Lady, to Prince" is from Jane Smiley, *Horse Heaven* (New York, Ballantine Books: 2000).

Acknowledgements

Thanks to the Canada Council for generous support.

Thanks to the editors of the following magazines in which some of these poems previously appeared: *PRISM international, Queen's Quarterly, Malahat Review, Fiddlehead, Event, New Quarterly, Lichen* and *Capilano Review.*

"Ma's Green Delaine Dress" appeared on-line in the *Guardian* (UK) Unlimited's May 2005 Poetry Workshop.

"Freddy, Dead at Nine Months" was shortlisted for *Prairie Fire*'s Bliss Carman Award, January 2005.

Selections from the book were shortlisted in 2003 and 2004 for the CBC Literary Awards.

A selection from the book was published in 2006 as a chapbook, *Switchgrass Stills*, by littlefishcartpress.

Thanks to Jeramy Dodds, Don McKay, A.F. Moritz, Sharon Thesen, Ross Leckie and the Ice House Poets for their insightful editorial attention. Thanks also to everyone at the Banff Centre for the Arts Writing Studio 2004 where many of these poems were written.

Love always to Mark.